Oxford Secondary English

Teacher's Book 3

John Seely

Oxford
University
Press
1982

Oxford University Press, Walton Street, Oxford OX2 6DP

London   Glasgow   New York   Toronto
Delhi   Bombay   Calcutta   Madras   Karachi
Nairobi   Dar es Salaam   Salisbury   Cape Town
Kuala Lumpur   Singapore   Hong Kong   Tokyo
Melbourne   Auckland

and associate companies in
Beirut   Berlin   Ibadan   Mexico City

© Oxford University Press 1982
ISBN 0 19 831138 9

Photoset in Great Britain by
Rowland Phototypesetting Ltd, Bury St Edmunds, Suffolk
and printed by Cambridge University Press, Cambridge.

Contents

Introduction

General

The best English teaching is done by teachers who know the children in their classes and choose materials and activities suited to their needs at the time. During any term their work together is very varied. This necessitates knowledge, experience, and sensitivity on the part of the teacher. It also requires time: time to think, to select, to prepare.

Unfortunately time is limited. This is particularly true for the teacher who is conscientious about reading and commenting on what his classes write. In addition, on many occasions teachers are asked to take responsibility for teaching English when it is not their specialist subject. For such 'part-time' English teachers the variety of possibilities and practice may seem bewildering.

In this course we have tried to offer a variety of materials in a form that will appeal to the children; but at the same time provide a structure that gives the teacher support, guidance, and choice in the business of organizing a coherent programme of work.

So, instead of the conventional one book per year, there are two: one for the pupils and one for the teacher. The pupil's book contains all the source materials plus some work assignments. The teacher's book contains most of the work assignments, as well as guidance on the use of the materials.

The books are divided into two sections. Section A, by far the larger, contains a selection of prose, poetry and visual material grouped into six themes. There are also three 'Specials'. Section B focusses on specific aspects of language in use and also contains a quick reference section on grammar, spelling, and punctuation.

The division into two sections is intended to give the teacher control over when to focus on language in a more direct and obvious way. If this language study material is contained in the thematic units, then it is difficult for him to do anything but use it when it occurs in a theme. If it is separated, as here, he can use it when he feels that the class is ready for it. In this part of the pupil's book each unit contains a variety of exercises. There is also a short reference section containing the main points of grammar, punctuation, and spelling, clearly set out. Pupils can refer to this when they want to check up on a point, or they can be directed to it in the case of error.

ANALYSIS OF THE MATERIALS

Pupil's Book

The pupil's book is divided into two sections:

1 Section A: 6 thematic units, averaging 16 pages each
   3 special units, averaging 16 pages each
2 Section B: 9 language in use units, averaging 3 pages each
   Reference section of 13 pages

Teacher's Book

The teacher's book is divided into three sections:

1 Introduction
2 Section A: Divided up in a similar way to the pupil's book, and containing the majority of the assignments on the material in the pupil's book, as well as a variety of teaching notes.
3 Section B: Short teaching notes on the materials in Section B of the pupil's book.

Using a Thematic Unit

Each thematic unit is arranged in a similar way. There are occasional minor variations from the pattern presented here. Each thematic unit is designed to contain sufficient material for up to four weeks' work.

Title: One or more illustrations introducing the theme as a whole. These can be used for a brief introductory discussion. A few discussion points are suggested either in the pupil's book or on the relevant page of the teacher's book.

Lead 'story': Usually a passage of prose fiction, but occasionally non-fiction or poetry, presenting the theme in a striking or dramatic way. It is followed by: *Questions to think and talk about*
Writing.

Development: One or two pages of contrasting material, followed by comprehension questions. The teacher's book often then contains supplementary comprehension material of different grades of difficulty enabling the text to be used by a wider ability spread. Since the Development pages extend the theme in a different direction from the Lead Story, they can be used immediately after it, or left until later in the work, or omitted.

Sources: A wide variety of prose, verse, and illustrations developing the theme. All activities based on this material are in the teacher's book. They are written in the form of direct address to the pupil and can therefore be used without further preparation by the teacher, who simply has to duplicate them, write on the blackboard, or just read them to the class. (For such purposes these exercises are cleared of copyright: see note at the beginning of this book.) There are also notes for the teacher. These are distinguished from exercise material by being printed in a different typeface.

This device frees the pupil's book for more source material. It leaves the teacher free to decide which material will be developed in detail. It frees the pupils from the requirements of a set of questions or writing assignments after everything they read. As a result, any parts of the source material can simply be read for pleasure.

Conclusion: At the end of each thematic unit there is a variety of material which is designed so that it can be used by pupils individually. Often this includes some simulation material, similar to that in the

'Specials' in Books 1 and 2. It often also contains other exercises based on the theme of the unit. This material will prove useful when the teacher wishes to set individual study, whether at school or at home. There are specific notes on the use of simulation material in each case, with suggestions on how it may be developed, if desired, for work in small groups. It is, however, written so that it can always be done individually.

Using the Special Units

Each of the three Special units is based on a different literary genre: short story, poetry, play. Each contains a considerable number of suggestions for activities by the class during and after their reading of the literature presented in the unit. The assignments in the pupil's book generally focus on the specific material that the unit contains and its broad themes. Those in the teacher's book pursue these lines further and also suggest ways in which the class can be introduced to the idea of literary genre – the ways in which the form of a piece of literature actually affects our understanding and appreciation of it. There are also suggestions of ways in which a start can be made on the more formal approaches that are generally demanded by examinations at 16+, since many teachers feel that the second half of the third year is not too early for a beginning to be made on such work.

Using Section B

The nine units of Section B are written for class teaching. The teacher's book contains suggestions for ways in which the material can be supplemented. In most cases the units are not really suitable for individual study, although some of them could well be tackled in groups with occasional sessions in which the class operates as a whole. Alternatively, class discussion could be combined with individual work on the exercises.

As suggested earlier, the Reference section is mainly intended for individual reference and revision, although of course it can be used with the class as a whole when it is necessary to reinforce a particular point.

SPECIFIC ACTIVITIES

Talking

One of the most important ways in which we learn is through talking and listening to other people. Speech is not just an important means of gathering and conveying information, it is a fundamental way in which our mental picture of the world is constantly being adjusted. In the past schools have failed to take full notice of this. In the traditional classroom most of the talking is done by the teacher while the pupils' role is to listen. As a result, most classrooms are still arranged in a way that discourages the kind of talk that leads to real learning. Such talk is exploratory, tentative, informal. The traditional classroom is designed for formal question-and-answer work.

This means that the teacher has to overcome a certain inertia if he is to have useful talk going on in his classroom. The problems that may exist can be set out thus:

Problems deriving from the school

1 Other teachers may disapprove: they may feel that talk is not 'work'.
2 Senior teachers may officially discourage talk, since they consider that it leads to disorder.
3 The arrangement of the classrooms may make informal talk difficult to get going.

Problems deriving from the teacher

4 He may worry that some children will 'take advantage' of the informality to misbehave.
5 He may feel that he cannot adequately monitor what is going on during informal talk.
6 He may feel under pressure to produce written work in every lesson.

Problems deriving from the pupils

7 If the method is little used in the school they may be uncertain of how to behave.
8 If the teacher seems unsure of himself they may reflect his nervousness in their classroom behaviour.

The teacher has to work within the school. He must decide for himself how best to cope with the prevailing 'official' opinion about talk. The remaining problems are more apparent than real. With determination, confidence and good planning, they can be overcome. It is possible to structure lessons in such a way that everyone knows clearly where he stands and what he has to do. Once he has started, the teacher will soon see the real benefits that the children are deriving from informal talk as these begin to spill over into all the other activities of English lessons.

Working in small groups

Without doubt the most effective method of organizing this kind of learning is in small groups. Initially a lot of very useful work can be done in pairs, with the teacher simply instructing members of the class to discuss the topic with the person they are sitting next to. Some pairs, however, do not get on, for one reason or another, so often a slightly larger group – of four or even, on occasions, five – proves more satisfactory in the long run. Such group discussion, when properly managed by the teacher, is in fact often more productive (and less wearing) than the more conventional class discussion with the teacher acting as chairman.

Arranging the groups

Some teachers simply tell the children to 'get into groups', allowing them to do so freely on a basis of friendship. Others go to the opposite extreme and construct elaborately artificial and balanced groups that take no account of the preferences of the children involved. Probably something between the two is the most successful: the children propose and the teacher disposes. Its organization may seem a little complicated, but is well worthwhile.

1   The teacher explains to the class what is going to be done: they will be working in small groups and they are to have some choice about whom they will work with.

2   Each child is given a piece of paper. He writes on it: his own name, followed by the names of the four people he would most like to work with in English. This is done without discussion, and in secrecy.

3   The teacher collects the papers which can then be used to guide his construction of the working groups. Children can be grouped mainly according to friendship (which is, after all a very important criterion) but the teacher can ensure that the groups are balanced in ability. He can also avoid having all the 'old lags' in one group.

4   At the next lesson the children are told their groups. Both they and the teacher have had a say in how the groups are made up. In theory at least, everyone is happy.

Organizing group work

The most important factor contributing to the success of small group discussion is simple, but often overlooked: every member of every group must have a very clear idea of what he is expected to do. This can be reduced to three questions:

1   How are we to organize ourselves?

2   Exactly what are we supposed to be talking about?

3   What is the outcome supposed to be?

In the early stages it is advisable to tell each group to appoint a chairman (or to appoint one yourself). The chairman's job is to ensure that the group sticks to the point and to resolve any disputes about whose turn it is to speak – if they are that sort of group.

Inexperienced groups find it helpful to have a list of topics or questions which are to be covered. The *Discussion points* in the teacher's book materials for Section A are presented with this in mind.

A simple way of monitoring group work 'in advance' is to tell the groups that after a given period they are going to have to report back to the rest of the class, either by giving their answers to a set of questions, or by reporting the conclusions they reached. Another role for the chairman can then be to record decisions.

This kind of formal organization is particularly useful early on. As children become accustomed to this method of working, it will often be found that there is no need for such a structure. Some classes, on the other hand, will always need it.

Monitoring

Teachers who are new to this kind of work are often uncertain of their own role once the discussion has begun. There are all the children busily talking away: what do I do now? How do I make sure that they aren't talking about something completely different? Such worries are usually unfounded (and illogical: after all, how do you make sure that any particular child is actually reading silently when he is supposed to be?). The way in which the teacher has set things up nearly always ensures that most of the time most of the children will be doing what he wants them to do. If they are not, then they are probably not just talking about something else, they are probably actively disrupting the rest of the class. In that case it is the teacher's relationship with the class that is at fault and not the teaching method itself.

If you do not know the class well, it is probably unhelpful to walk round and try to join in particular discussions. It is better to choose two or three 'observation points' in the room from which you can 'tune in' to the talk of the groups around you, without making it particularly obvious that you are doing so. When you do know the class well, it is both valuable and enjoyable to be able to join in particular discussions.

The teacher's most important function, however, is probably to assess how the session as a whole is going. He needs to be able to judge when the talk is beginning to flag and to intervene, either by bringing things to a conclusion or by introducing some new element. This is the most difficult thing to learn about managing group discussion.

Working with the whole class
Some teachers will prefer to work fairly frequently, or even all the time, with the class as a whole. Those who do should try to achieve the best elements of small-group discussion in their work with the class.

1 *The role of the teacher*
He should avoid being too 'heavy' and should encourage children to talk directly to each other rather than always speaking 'through' him. Ideally he should just be there to cue in individuals who are looking for a chance to contribute.

2 *Informality*
As far as possible it is important to avoid the heavily structured pattern of teacher-talks-class-listen-then-pupil-answers-teacher-comments. This is partly done by the teacher disciplining himself to listen to what children actually say, rather than looking for what he thinks they ought to be saying. It is helped by not interrupting children more often than necessary. Most of all it is done by the teacher keeping quiet.

3 *Participation*
The aim should always be to have as many children as possible actively participating. It is a useful (and sobering) exercise after a class discussion for the teacher to ask himself:
a For what proportion of the total time was *I* talking?
b What percentage of the children spoke?

(This is not to say that just because a child does not speak he is not participating. There is such a thing as active listening.)

Using the materials

Every unit of Section A contains three types of material that can lead to oral work.

1 *Questions about a passage or poem*

The Lead Story questions are always of this kind. Other sets of questions in the teacher's book may be suitable. Such material can be used for group work or taken with the class as a whole.

2 *Discussion points*

These are particularly useful as guidelines for small group discussion, but they can also be used with the class together.

3 *Group work*

Here the instructions in the teacher's book are written in the form of address *to groups*. It is usually difficult or impossible to use this material in any other way.

Drama

The drama materials contained in Section A of the teacher's book do not in themselves provide a sustained or coherent programme of work in drama for a year. They are not intended to. They are designed to supplement work already being done in drama, whether by the English teacher or by a drama specialist. Teachers who are inexperienced in this type of work and who feel that they would like to begin it, are recommended to use some of the materials in *Dramakit* (John Seely, Oxford University Press).

Every thematic unit does contain one or more items of drama work. They take various forms:

Role-play: in which the participants are invited to take on social roles in a situation related to the theme. In such situations, the participants can still use quite a lot of their own personalities – they do not have to go very far towards constructing a 'character'.

Playmaking: in which instructions are given (normally for groups) explaining how to set about constructing one or more scenes expressing a reaction to a situation, character or theme. Such scenes may or may not ultimately be shared with the rest of the class.

'Radio' plays: from time to time either role-play work (especially on interviews) or script-writing exercises lead naturally on to the construction of 'radio' plays. If there are enough tape recorders available then plays can be recorded, which is clearly the most satisfactory arrangement. If not, then the plays can be prepared for a live performance.

There are, too, occasionally suggestions for the organization of more complex and detailed drama lessons. In these cases specific advice is provided for the teacher.

Contents

TWO SIDES TO EVERYTHING

* Pupil's Book page
** Teacher's book page

1

Analysis of activities

Discussion: 1   2   3   T4   T6   T7
Writing: personal   3
       about people   3
       dialogue   5   18
       narrative   T4   T7
       argument/exposition   18   T4
       different viewpoints   T7
       letter   18
       criticism   T6
       poetry   T6
Comprehension: 5   T5
Criticism: T3
Research: 18   T3
Group work: T7   T8
Simulation: T8

Illustrations

Pupil's book page 1   research

Research

Look through old newspapers and magazines. Find contrasting pairs of pictures like those on this page. Cut them out and stick them into your book. Underneath each pair explain why you chose it and in what way you think it shows that there are 'two sides to everything'.

My busconductor

Pupil's book page 2   criticism

Comparisons

The poem contains a number of comparisons:

> He holds a ninepenny single
> as if it were a rose.

A rose is something beautiful and when we hold one we treat it with great care because it is something we care about. Roger McGough thinks that this is how the busconductor holds tickets now that he knows he is going to die. So he compares the two.

Write down the other comparisons in the poem and explain why you think the poet used them.

She's leaving home

Pupil's book page 6   writing

Writing

The song doesn't tell the whole story. It leaves a lot of questions unanswered. What happens next? Does the girl stay away, or does she return? Do the parents try to trace her and persuade her to come home? Decide for yourself how the story ends and then, in your own words, tell the whole story.

Alternatively, see the suggestion for a group play on the same material on page T5.

The Parents' Charter

Pupil's book page 7 discussion; writing

Discussion points

1 What are people's 'rights'?
2 Why do people have rights?
3 Do children have any rights? Why?
4 What should a Children's Charter contain?
5 Do parents have rights?
6 What should their Charter contain?

Writing

Write a Charter of Rights for one of the following groups:

  children
  parents
  pupils
  teachers
  traffic wardens
  newspaper boys/girls

  or any group of your choice.

Jerusalem

comprehension;
drama

These sets of comprehension questions are in ascending order of difficulty.

Comprehension

Questions A
1 What does Sammy want to do?
2 Why?
3 How does Dave feel about this?
4 Why?

Questions B
1 Where does Dave come from?
2 Where does Sammy come from?
3 What is Dave's view of living in the country?
4 How does Sammy feel about living in the country?
5 What is Dave's opinion about working in a factory?
6 What is Sammy's opinion?

Questions C
1 Dave has a long speech at the bottom of page 8 beginning, 'That I do not have an answer to . . .' What is he trying to explain to Sammy in the speech?
2 What arguments does Dave put forward in favour of the life that he and Sammy lead at the moment? (Look particularly at his speech on page 9 beginning, 'But that's not all, cocker . . .')
3 How does Sammy answer him?
4 Who do you think has the better argument and why?

Group playmaking

Read *She's Leaving Home* and *Jerusalem* and choose one of them as the basis for a group play.
1 Read the chosen piece again, carefully.
2 Discuss the story it tells. Neither piece tells the whole of a story, so you will have to decide what you think the rest of the story is.
3 Decide how many scenes the story divides into.
4 For each scene, decide: *when* and *where* it happens and *who* the main characters are.
5 Cast the parts.
6 Work through each scene in improvization. Don't try to plan the scenes too carefully. Just decide roughly what happens and how the scene starts. Then go through it, making it up as you go along.
7 After you have improvized the whole story, discuss it and decide how it should be altered and improved.
8 Now practise the scenes, including the changes you have decided on.

The School Boy

Pupil's book page **10**   discussion

Questions to think and talk about
1   What does the schoolboy love doing?
2   What is his school like?
3   He compares schoolchildren to two different things. What are they and why does he make the comparison?
4   What effects does he say school has on children?
5   Blake lived about two hundred years ago. Do you think what he says has any truth for today?

Discussion points
Many writers have made criticisms of school that are similar to Blake's, but what is the alternative? What would our society be like if

    a   there were no schools at all?

or **b** everyone had to pay school fees if they wanted to attend school?

or **c** only a few people were allowed to attend school after the age of 11?

Schoolmaster

Pupil's book page **11**   criticism; writing

Writing about the poem
Write a short paragraph in answer to each of these questions.
1   In this poem we see the children gradually sympathizing with the teacher. Explain in your own words how and why this happens.
2   How did *you* feel at the end of the poem, and why?

Writing from inside the poem
The poem is 'told' by a pupil in the class. Imagine that you are the pupil. When you get home that day, you tell your family about 'What happened in Maths today'.

Your own writing
Look at the two poems *The School Boy* and *Schoolmaster*. The first was written almost two hundred years ago, and the second is by a contemporary Russian poet. Write two contrasting poems or descriptions with the same titles but about this country today.

Scenes from a bomber raid

Pupil's book pages **12–16**   discussion; writing; group work

Discussion points

These extracts give us a number of different viewpoints of one event in the war. How do you think each of these characters felt about the bombing raid?

The Group Captain
Jammy Giles
The telephonist
Bodo Reuter

Writing

In *Bomber* Len Deighton builds up a very comprehensive picture of one event, a bombing raid on a German town during the Second World War. He does this by putting together hundreds of small details. He writes from both British and German points of view. The raid is seen through the eyes of many different British and German people involved. The extracts show how it works.

Write a story that is built up in the same way. Choose your own subject matter, or take one of these suggestions.

topic	viewpoints
1 A street accident	drivers, pedestrians, police, relatives, ambulance men, nurses, doctors.
2 A flood	weather forecasters, coastguards, local people, families, officials, police, rescue workers.
3 A fire	the person(s) who started it, the person who gave the alarm, people in the building, people in the street, firemen, nurses and ambulance men, the policemen, reporters.

The writing exercise can be done individually or in small groups. In groups the work begins with a period of discussion and planning. A story line is worked out. The viewpoints are selected. They are then divided among the members of the group. Each writes his own section(s) of the story. The group then reassembles to select and edit the story as a whole.

The brewery site

Pupil's book pages **17–18**

simulation; group work

Instead of being used as an individual writing exercise, this material can be developed into a full-scale simulation. The class is asked to decide how many different groups of people might have an interest in this problem: residents, ratepayers, local officials, conservationists, police, parents, schools etc. These groups are then 'cast' from the class, so that everyone has a role. The groups then meet and discuss how they will present their case. They manufacture any documents they need. There is then a 'Public Enquiry', chaired by the teacher, in which each group is given a chance to air its views.

A follow-up exercise can then be done in which newspapers (and possibly local radio) report on the Enquiry and its findings.

Contents

Rites and Ceremonies

* Pupil's book page
** Teacher's book page

Analysis of activities

Discussion: 19 21 T11 T12 T13 T14 T17
Writing: narrative 21 T14
       in role T14
       images T16
Comprehension: 23 T12 T18
Criticism: T16
Language study: T12
Research: 33 T13
Project: T11
Drama: T14

Illustrations

Pupil's book page **19**   discussion; project

1   State funeral of Winston Churchill
2   Bar Mitzvah ceremony
3   Birthday party
4   Indonesian sunset ceremony
5   Crowning the bard

Discussion
A discussion of these pictures can lead into a more general consideration
of the part played by rites and ceremonies in our lives. The class can be
asked to list other ceremonies in which they have participated or about
which they know.

Project
As you work on this unit, make a collection of other examples of rites and
ceremonies. These can be:
1   short descriptions
2   cuttings from newspapers or magazines
3   pictures

Meeting Kondén Diara

Pupil's book pages **20–1**   comprehension;
discussion

Comprehension
Write a paragraph, explaining in your own words what the ritual of
meeting Kondén Diara consisted of. Ignore the writer's feelings: simply
describe what happened.

Group discussion
Read the passage carefully. Discuss how the elders and the older boys
organized the ordeal of meeting Kondén Diara.

Initiation among the Amazon Indians

Pupil's book pages **22–3**　　　　　　　　　　comprehension

Comprehension
The following additional exercises may be used to supplement the set of questions in the pupil's book. Set A are easier than those in the pupil's book: Set B are more difficult.

Questions A
1　At what age does the Carib girl's initiation take place?
2　How long does it take?
3　The ceremony uses two special things. What are they?
4　How old are Panare boys when they are initiated?
5　What is the most important part of their initiation?

Questions B
1　Many initiation rites contain actions that symbolize or stand for something else. In what ways is the Carib girl's initiation *symbolic*?
2　What symbols are used in the Panare boys' ceremony?
3　Write a paragraph explaining the ways in which the initiation of Carib girls and Panare boys is similar.
4　Write a paragraph explaining the main ways in which the ceremonies are different.

Church wedding

Pupil's book pages **24–5**　　　　　　discussion; writing; language study

Questions to think and talk about
Read the two extracts carefully. Then think about the answers to these questions.
1　Are there any parts of the 1662 ceremony that you find difficult to understand or follow? If so, what are they?
2　Are there any parts of the 1980 ceremony that you find difficult to understand or follow? If so, what are they?
3　Do you think that the 1980 version is more suitable for use today than the 1662 version? If so, why? If not, why not?

Language study
1　In what ways do you think language has changed between the seventeenth and the twentieth centuries? Can you find examples in these extracts?
2　Make a detailed comparison of the two extracts. List words and

Church wedding *continued*

discussion; writing;
language study

phrases that illustrate the changes that have been made. Do it like this:

1662	1980
thee	you
to my wedded wife	to be my wife
ordinance	law

etc.

3 Certain words and phrases have not changed:

a to have and to hold
b for better, for worse
c for richer, for poorer
d in sickness and in health
e to love and to cherish
f till death us do part

i Write down what you think each of these means.
ii Would you say that these phrases are still 'modern' English?
iii Why have they not been changed?

4 The 1980 version of the Marriage Service was written to make sure that its meaning was clear to those who used it. Do you think it succeeds in doing this? What are your reasons?

Discussion

Many people who do not normally go to church still choose to get married in church. If they are members of the Church of England, then they probably use the 1980 service.

1 Why do so many people still like to get married in church?
2 Do you think they should, if they are not normally church-goers?
3 The words of the 1980 service are still quite complicated and difficult. Many of them still go back to the seventeenth century. Do the actual words we use matter that much?
4 Wouldn't it be better to use simpler words and have a shorter service?
5 Can you think of any other occasions when people use special words and phrases because of the importance of what they are talking about?

Research

A Find out the words of another marriage service – of a civil (Registry Office) ceremony; or of another Christian denomination; or of another religion.

Compare this service with the 1980 service extract. What are the main similarities and differences?

B Choose some other ceremony in which words play an important part. Find out as much about it as you can. Write a description of it. Explain the part that special words play in the ceremony.

'Blackie, The Electric Rembrandt'

Pupil's book page **26**   discussion; writing;
                                                             drama

Questions to think and talk about

1   Who else is mentioned in the poem apart from Blackie and the boy
    who is being tattooed?
2   Why are they there?
3   What do they share with Blackie?
4   Why does the boy not look at Blackie's hand?
5   Why is he holding his breath?
6   How do you think he feels at the end of the poem?
7   What is the meaning of the title of the poem?

Group discussion

For some people tattoos are a kind of membership badge to a group. For
other groups the membership badge is not a tattoo but something else: a
hairstyle, a way of talking, special clothes.

1   Make a list of groups that you can think of that have this kind of
    'badge'.
2   Why do they have this kind of 'badge'?
3   If the badge is something that can be changed – like clothes – do
    people behave differently when they are wearing it, from when they
    are not? If so, why?
4   How do the members of these groups feel about people who do not
    belong?

Writing

You have just joined a group of people. The sign of membership is a
particular hairstyle, or special clothes, or something else that makes it
quite clear you are a member of that group. Tell the story of what
happens on the first day you go home 'wearing' this 'membership
badge'.

Drama

The following improvization is for groups of three or four.

1   Choose one of the following extracts of conversation.
2   Discuss the extract. Decide: how many people speak; who they are;
    what they are talking about; where and when the conversation takes
    place; how the conversation starts.
3   Give each member of the group a part.
4   Decide how your scene begins.
5   Get into positions to start the scene, and, when everyone is ready,
    improvize the scene.
6   When you have finished the scene, discuss how it went. How true to
    life was it? How could it be improved?

'Blackie, The Electric Rembrandt' *continued*

discussion; writing
drama

7 Run through the scene again, making these improvements.

Note: there is no need to use the exact words printed – just the gist of
what is said.

A 'What on earth have you done to your hair?'
'Don't you like it?'
'It's disgusting.'
'I think it's rather nice.'
'Get out! Go on – get out!'

B 'You're not wearing that in here.'
'Why not?'
'I'm not having a daughter(son) of mine wearing clothes like that.
Over my dead body.'
'What a waste of money!'

Gunpowder Plot

Pupil's book page 27

Criticism

A   Impressions

1   How would you describe the mood of the first four verses?
2   How does this mood change towards the end of the poem?
3   Why does it change?
4   What do the fireworks mean to the children?
5   What do they mean to the person telling the story?

B   Words and images

1   Why are the fireworks described as 'curious cardboard buds'?
2   A phoenix was a mythical bird that was supposed to set itself on fire and then be reborn from the ashes, every five hundred years. Why, in verse 3, does he call the guy an 'absurdly human phoenix'?
3   What is he describing in these words:

> '. . . the harvest sky
> Is flecked with threshed and glittering golden grain.'

Why does he describe it in this way?
4   In verses 4 and 5 the word cannon has two different meanings – one to the children, the other to their uncle. What are these meanings?
5   What does he mean in verse 6 by '*taste* my fear'?

C   Seeing and hearing

The poem helps us to see and hear the fireworks and the wartime memory.

1   Choose three examples of words or phrases that help you to see what is being described.
2   Write them down and explain why you chose them.
3   Choose two examples of words and phrases that help you to hear what is being described.
4   Write them down and explain why you chose them.

Writing: images

> '. . . the frenzied whizz of Catherine-wheel
> Puts forth its fiery petals . . .'

By this image the writer helps us to hear and see the Catherine-wheel: he compares it to a flower made of fire. Write short descriptive images for any three of the following:

a waterfall	a traffic jam
a jet plane flying	a motorway pile-up
low overhead	a busy building site
a thunderstorm	a very angry man

The Law of Life

discussion

Questions to think and talk about

1 Who is Old Koskoosh?
2 Why is he only watching them strike camp and not helping?
3 Why does the writer describe in detail all the *sounds* of striking camp?
4 Why does it say (on page 30), 'At last the measure of his life was a handful of faggots'?
5 How would you describe Old Koskoosh's feelings as he waits?
6 What is 'The Law of Life'?

Group discussion

What Jack London describes in this story is a traditional custom of some American Indian tribes.

1 Why did they treat old people like this?
2 What does it tell us about their attitude to life and death?
3 Would you describe this custom as cruel, primitive, practical, or . . . what?
4 How do you think the members of this tribe would have thought about the way old people are treated in our society?

New every morning

Pupil's book pages **31–2**   comprehension

Comprehension

Questions A
1 Why is Mr Gryce so angry?
2 What happens to end the silence?
3 Who is caught and taken out of the hall?
4 Why does Mr Gryce stop the hymn?
5 How do the boys sing verse 2?
6 How does the boy who reads the lesson feel?

Questions B
1 Describe the arrangement of boys and teachers in the hall.
2 What was Mr Gryce's voice like when he first spoke?
3 How did the teachers feel about Mr Gryce?
4 What will happen to MacDowall?
5 How do the boys sing the first verse of the hymn?
6 How does Gryce say the words, 'Or I'll make you sing like you've never sung before.'
7 What effect does it have?

Questions C
1 Write a few sentences describing the character of Mr Gryce.
2 Write a few sentences giving your impressions of his school.

These three sets of questions are graded in ascending order of difficulty.

A calendar of festivals

Pupil's book page **33**   notes

Missing festivals
Shrove Tuesday	February/March before Ash Wednesday
St George's Day	23rd April
Pesach	March/April before Good Friday
Diwali	October/November

Jumbled story

Pupil's book page **34**   answers

The correct order is: 4–2–7–6–3–5–1.

Ted Hughes

A poet talks about poetry

Pupil's book pages **35–54**

This unit takes a more conscious look at the process of writing poetry than has been done elsewhere in the course. It does so by concentrating on the work of one poet, a writer who has devoted considerable time and energy to thinking about the process of writing and discussing this in a way that is accessible to people at school. The unit contains two prose extracts from talks originally given by Ted Hughes for the BBC *Listening and Writing* programmes and later published in *Poetry in the Making*. There are also six poems.

The unit falls into the following sections:

1 *Capturing Animals*: a prose passage about the poetic imagination followed by *Imagining*, a page of writing activities based on photographs.

2 *Learning to think*: a prose extract about the role of concentration in the process of writing poetry, followed by *Concentrating and Writing*, further activities and an illustration.

3 *Leaves* and *There came a day*, two pattern poems about Autumn from Hughes' collection *Season Songs*. These are followed by suggestions about writing similar poems.

4 *Hands* and *A Memory*: two poems from *Moortown*, again followed by suggestions about writing along similar lines.

Although pupils could be set to read any of these sections and then to do their own writing along the lines suggested, without any further assistance, it is probably more useful to work through each section with the class. The first two sections contain a large amount of material which will benefit from being discussed with the class. The particular ideas which Hughes explores can then be expanded as required. Discussion will also be useful in the third section, particularly in developing ideas for patterns which can be used for the pupils' own poems. The two poems in the fourth section are more difficult than the remainder of the poems in the unit. Most pupils should be able to gain a good idea of the general subject matter and approach in both, but the skilful use of discussion techniques will help to bring out the depth and quality of the poet's feelings towards the subject of the two poems.

In the suggestions for pupils' own writing, we have deliberately avoided asking the reader to write a 'poem'. Naturally we hope that on most occasions this will be attempted, but it is always open to the pupil to write a passage of imaginative prose instead.

For those who wish to develop this work further, these books may prove useful:

Hughes, T.   *Poetry in the Making* (Faber)
Fairfax, J., Moat, J.   *The Way to Write* (Elm Tree Books)

Contents

* Pupil's book page
**Teacher's book page

Analysis of activities

Discussion: 55   58   T22   T24   T26   T28
Writing: personal   58
         story   58
         ballad   T23
         radio play   T23
         in character   70
         newspaper report   70
         argument   70
         simulation   70
Comprehension: 59   T24
Research: T28
Group work: T28
Drama: T28

Illustration

Pupil's book page 55   discussion

The painting is *The Scream* by Edvard Munch. Pupils may well have seen it before and may already have formed strong opinions about it. Even if they have not it is such a powerful work that a first sight of it will often provoke considerable discussion. The talk that ensues could be guided to consider the following questions:

1   What was your immediate reaction on seeing this picture?
2   What emotion do you think this person is experiencing?
3   What do you think the reasons for it are?
4   What do you think the situation is – what about the two figures behind the main character?
5   Why do you think the painter painted it?

Cruel and unfair

Pupil's book pages 56–8   discussion

The passage will often benefit from a brief introduction by the teacher. In particular the salient features which made Stephen's school strange or different were that it was: single sex, a Roman Catholic School run mainly by priests and brothers, one where physical punishment was used more than it is today. It is also confusing that at this school a 'prefect' was a teacher and not a pupil – moreover a teacher who was purely responsible for disciplinary matters.

Further discussion may focus on: the question of whether unfair, or apparently unfair treatment by a school or other social institution may turn a person into an outsider; the rightness or wrongness of corporal punishment in schools; and the power wielded in general by school-teachers.

Pretty Boy Floyd

Pupil's book page **59**   writing

Writing a ballad

Pretty Boy Floyd is a ballad. A ballad is a poem that tells a story. It is usually written in verses four lines long. Usually the lines rhyme. In this ballad the second and fourth lines rhyme in most verses. Ballads are often sung rather than spoken, so they have a fairly regular beat, or rhythm.

Write a ballad about one of your own heroes. Follow the same pattern as *Pretty Boy Floyd*. Don't worry too much about the rhyming – Woodie Guthrie didn't. (Verses 2 and 8 don't rhyme at all.)

Writing a radio play

Use *Pretty Boy Floyd* as the basis for a radio play about the outlaw. Divide the story into sections and introduce each section with part of the ballad.

Example

NARRATOR: Others tell you 'bout a stranger
That came to beg a meal,
And underneath his napkin
Left a thousand-dollar bill.

Action: A farming family are just sitting down to supper when there is a knock at the door. It is Floyd. He begs the farmer to give him some food. He is invited in to share the family meal. When he has finished he thanks them for their kindness and goes on his way. When they are clearing the table, they find a thousand-dollar bill hidden under his napkin.

Note: you will find advice on how to set out a script on page 183.

A menace to society

Pupil's book pages 60–1

Discussion points

1 What is the point of sending people to prison?
2 Keeping someone in prison costs as much as keeping him in a good hotel. Is it worth it?
3 Are there any alternatives? If so, what are they?
4 Bill Fletcher argues that prison actually makes people worse. Is he right? If so, what can be done about it?
5 If you had been the judge at Hereford, what sentence would you have given Bill Fletcher?

The comprehension questions that follow are graded. Set A are the simplest and Set C the most difficult. They are about different sections of the story. They can be given to the class as three separate sets of questions, or as one complete set of twenty.

Questions A

All these questions are based on the last part of the story, section D. Answer them in your own words.

1 What did Bill Fletcher decide 'two years ago'?
2 So what did he do?
3 Why?
4 Where was he sent to be sentenced?
5 What kind of sentence did he want?
6 What sentence did he get?
7 Why did the judge do that?

Questions B

All these questions are based on section C of the story. Answer them in your own words.

1 In what circumstances is a prisoner given new clothes?
2 What else is he given?
3 When he gets out of prison what is the first thing he finds unusual?
4 'Within an hour you feel a nervous wreck . . .' Why?
5 Why does the prisoner look for a shop where there is a man serving?
6 Why has Bill Fletcher never bought himself new clothes?
7 What reason does he give to explain why many prisoners keep returning to prison?

Questions C
All these questions are based on section B of the story. Answer them in your own words.

1   Explain what each of these words means, as it is used in the story:
      sadism   craft   record
2   What criminal skill did Bill Fletcher learn at Borstal?
3   Why does he say he had to become a thief at approved school?
4   Why is he still frightened of the authorities?
5   How did Dartmoor make him feel?
6   What does he mean by the sentence, 'What I learnt most of all was a dread of the human race'?

In Coventry   I am

Pupil's book pages 62–3   discussion

These poems are not easy. Just how far one attempts to go with them depends very much on the class. The notes that are provided on the next page may prove useful with some classes, but many readers will be able to get a good intuitive grasp of the poems without digging around too much into what particular words and phrases mean.

In Coventry

Coventry was heavily bombed and very badly damaged during the Second World War. The old cathedral was almost completely destroyed. After the war a new city and a new cathedral arose from the ruins.

1 Which parts of the new cathedral did Charles Causley particularly notice?
2 What was the first thing that drew his attention to the man?
3 Why did the man fall over?
4 What did the man's friends do?
5 What happened to the man later?
6 What impression does the poem give you of Coventry and its cathedral?

I am

John Clare lived in the Northamptonshire countryside. He was born in 1793 and died in 1864. He worked as a labourer. He had a great love of the countryside and wrote poems about the things he saw around him. Some of his poems were published and for a while he became quite famous. It did not last, however, and he remained poor. He became increasingly depressed and eventually so ill that he was taken into Northampton Lunatic Asylum, where he wrote many poems, including this one.

1 What feelings does he express in verse 1?
2 What does he feel about his friends and family (verse 2)?
3 What does he dream of (verse 3)?

Notes on *In Coventry/I am*

In Coventry

Line 1   *ruddled:* marked with red – presumably a reference to the bombing of Coventry and the bloodshed caused.

     5/6   these lines refer to the Graham Sutherland tapestry illustrated on the same page as the poem.

     7/8   At the entrance to the chapel there is a large metal crown of thorns, which was made in the workshops of the Royal Engineers.

     10   *retablos:* decorative panels.

     19   *chunnered:* presumably the same as 'chuntered' – muttered or grumbled.

I am

Line 3   *self-consumer of my woes:* stressing the fact that Clare felt that only he experienced and understood his own unhappiness.

    4   *oblivious* means 'unaware of anything else' — it can refer to the sorrows (which disregard everything else) or Clare himself, who is made oblivious of everything else by the sorrows.

    5   *oblivion:* forgetfulness.

    6   *tost:* tossed.

    10   Clare's career had been promising and now lies in ruins.

    18   *vaulted:* arched.

Extra lesson

Pupil's book pages **64–6**   discussion; research

Discussion point
What do you think of the way Herr Neudorf behaved?

Research
Prejudice is often accompanied by ignorance. Choose a group of people against whom there is hostility or prejudice. (It may be because of their religion or other beliefs; their race; their occupation; or for some other reason.) Find out as much as you can about them and why it is that there are these feelings against them. How do you think they feel about the hostility they experience? Try to find out something about their points of view. Write a report on what you have found out and the conclusions that you draw.

Story kit: Ned Kelly

Pupil's book pages **67–70**   group work; drama

General
These four pages are written so that they can be used either by individuals or by small groups.

Group work
There are general comments on small group activities on pages viii-ix of the *Introduction*. If this section is done in small groups, the writing activities are preceded by a period of discussion and pooling of ideas. After this, the writing task(s) can be divided among the group and the writing work itself done individually.

Drama
The story of Ned Kelly can also be presented in dramatic form. Groups can improvize selected incidents from his life and then rehearse these for presentation. The dramatization can be given a more formal structure by using a ballad narration, or the trial situation, or the argument suggestion in activity number 5. Dramatization provides a stimulus for further research, since the details given in the pupil's book are inevitably limited.

Contents

Money, money, money

* Pupil's book page
** Teacher's book page

Analysis of activities

Discussion: 71   73   75   T31   T32   T33
Writing: narrative   73   T35
          satirical   T33
          advertisements   86
          report   86
          description   T34
          critical   T33   T34   T36
          letter   T35
          character description   T36
Comprehension: 75   86
Criticism: satire   T33
          background   T34
          mood/emotion   T34
          character   T36
Drama: T34
Research/projects: 86   T31   T32

Illustrations

Pupil's book page **71**   discussion

These questions can be used to amplify and develop those in the pupil's book.

Discussion points

1   Do you think that all people should be paid the same, regardless of their jobs?
2   If so, why?
3   If so, what about people who are lazy: should *they* be paid less? Who is to decide who is 'lazy'?
4   If people doing different jobs should be paid different amounts, how can this be decided fairly? What standards can be used: difficulty, unpleasantness, importance?
5   What other factors, apart from money, can make a job attractive?
6   If a job is attractive and interesting because of these factors should it be paid less?

Ambition

Pupil's book pages **72–3**   project

Solo or group project
Many of Joe's ideas about the kind of lifestyle he would like to have come from advertising and films. Since *Room at the Top* was written, things have changed. A modern Joe Lampton would aspire to different things. Make a selection of advertisements and magazine pictures to illustrate the kind of 'life at the top' that Joe might aim for today. Present these as a wall display or folder.

Growing up in the 1920s

discussion; research

Questions to think and talk about

A

1 Are there people as poor as this in Britain today?
2 Are there many people in Britain today whom you would describe as poor?
3 If so, what are the reasons for their poverty?
4 What do you think are the main improvements that have taken place since the 1920s?
5 Many people believe that everyone has the 'right' to a 'living wage'. What do you think they mean by a 'living wage'?
6 Would you agree with them? Why should it be a 'right'?

B

In large areas of the world, people still live in conditions like those described in the passage – or even worse. In our society this is very rare. The gap between rich and poor countries is widening.

1 Is this fair?
2 Can anything be done about it?
3 Does it matter?

Research

Find out about voluntary organizations that help poor people in Britain and overseas.

1 Make a list of their names.
2 Collect copies of their advertisements.
3 Find out as much as you can about each one.
4 Present your research in your exercise book, or in a special folder, describing what you have found out and illustrating it with advertisements and pictures from magazines.

Money madness   Wages

Pupil's book page 76   discussion

Questions to think and talk about

Money madness
1   What does Lawrence mean by 'bread', 'shelter', and 'fire'?
2   Why does he think they should be free?
3   Do you think he is right?

Wages
4   What do you think Lawrence means by the first four lines?
5   What is a 'vicious circle'?
6   Is he right to say that the more people get the more they want (lines 5 and 6)?
7   What does he mean by saying that being a wage earner is like being in prison?
8   Is he right?
9   What does he mean by the last line?

Song of the man who has money

Pupil's book page 77   criticism; writing

Thinking and writing about the poem

In this poem, Arthur Hugh Clough is writing a *satire*. This means that he is attacking something he hates by making fun of it.
1   To do this, he pretends to be a certain kind of person. Describe that kind of person.
2   He rejoices in the things that money enables him to do. Name some of them.
3   What attitude does he show towards poor people in verses 1 and 2?
4   What attitude does he show towards poor people in the last verse?
5   What does the poem make you feel about the narrator ('I')?

Writing

The poem satirizes a set of attitudes. It does this by describing a person who shows them in a very exaggerated form. Write a modern satire in verse or prose on one of the following:

The man who has money
The pop or football fan
The man of prejudice

The people race

Group drama

1   Discuss the different ways in which people compete with each other over material possessions: in which they 'try to keep up with the Joneses'. Think of as many different examples of this as you can.

2   Now make up a series of short conversations for two or three people illustrating how absurd this kind of competition can be.

3   Make up a series of short scenes about the same two families who compete with each other in order to 'keep up'. This can start with quite small, simple things, like the colour of their front curtains, and gradually build up until the two families are competing about very large things which are quite absurd.

4   Now select from what you have done and make up a short programme entitled 'The Joneses'. Practise this for performance to the class, or for recording on a cassette recorder.

Wealth

Appreciation

A   Understanding the story

If you read the passage carefully, you can build up a clear picture in your mind of the kind of country in which Kino and his family lived. Write a short description of it. Include information on the following points:

the way of life of Kino and his family;

how Kino and the other men earned their living;

the kind of place in which they lived;

who the rich people were and how they were rich;

the attitudes of all these people to money.

B   Reading with imagination

As we read the story we can see that the finding of the pearl has a different effect on all the people described. In particular they all experience different thoughts and feelings. Write a paragraph describing how the discovery of the pearl makes them feel. You should mention the following characters:

the pearl buyers

Kino

Juana

the village people

Wealth *continued*

C   Speculating about the story

There is a particular atmosphere about this story. How would you describe it? How do you think the story ends? Why?

Your own writing

You have won a modern 'pearl of the world': decide what it is. It might be the football pools, a lottery, a big Premium Bond prize. Decide how much it is.

A   Preparatory work

1   Just before the results are announced, you think about what you would do if you won the big prize. Write down the thoughts you have.

2   The results are announced and you have won. Describe your feelings at that moment.

3   You discuss your win with your family and friends. How do they react? Write the conversation.

4   The news gets out that you have won this money. Everybody wants to be your friend: even people you have hardly spoken to before. What happens when they talk to you? Describe it.

5   You begin to receive begging letters from people whom you have never met, asking you to give them money. Write such a letter and then describe how you respond to it.

B   Writing the story

The preparatory work should have given you a lot of material to use in your story. Now write the story of your 'Big Win'. Use some or all of the material you wrote during the preparatory work. Give your story a clear ending.

The miser

Pupil's book pages **81–2**   writing; criticism

Writing: borrowing a character
Read the description of Scrooge carefully. Try to imagine what he looked like; how he moved; how he spoke. When you have got a clear picture of him in your head, write a description of a meeting between him and someone else in a modern setting: a meeting that takes place today. As Scrooge and this other person meet, they talk – write their conversation. Either choose the character that Scrooge meets from the list that follows, or invent one.

his bank manager
a charity collector (decide which charity)
someone selling programmes for the local carnival
someone selling something at the door (decide what)

Criticism: character description
In this passage, Dickens uses a number of different ways of describing the character of Scrooge.

Appearance
He tells us what Scrooge looked like.
1   Make a list of some of the words he uses to describe the appearance of Scrooge.
2   Write a description of what he looks like, using your own words.

Comparison
He uses a lot of comparisons to give us a clear idea of what Scrooge was like. In particular he compares him with the weather.
3   Explain what you think each of these comparisons means:
      'Hard and sharp as flint . . .'
      'He carried his own low temperature always about with him . . .'
4   Find two more comparisons and explain what they mean.

Contrast
He contrasts Scrooge with his nephew.
5   Read this part of the passage again.
6   How does this conversation tell us more about Scrooge?

The cost of living

Pupil's book pages **83–6**   organization

The materials on these four pages can be used with the class as a whole, worked on in groups, or individually. The results of writing and research assignments can be presented as wall displays, folders or booklets.

The Wedge-tailed Eagle

Pupil's book pages 87–96

General
There is always a danger, when reading and discussing a story that deals explicitly with violence, that the activity will be counter-productive: that in seeking to examine and understand why people do things that are senseless and cruel, we will merely confirm and strengthen tendencies towards violence that already exist. On the other hand, we cannot just shut our eyes to violence and hope it will go away. This story contains a valid examination of thoughtless violence, set within a sensitive and implicitly moral framework. The descriptive language is poetic; the action is complex and dramatic; and the conclusion invites a moral judgement.

Introducing the story
For the reasons suggested above, the story may well need some kind of general introduction. This does, however, very much depend on the class. If the teacher is confident that an unintroduced reading will not produce the counter-reaction suggested earlier, then there is no need for detailed preliminary work.

An introduction could contain some or all of the following elements:

a Discussion of pests and how they should be treated. What makes an animal a pest? What gives man the right to 'put them down'? What gives man the right to kill any animals? Is a creature like a household fly (i.e. ugly and insignificant) more of a pest than, say, a coypu? (Or a nice, furry bunny rabbit?)

b Discussion of animals and sport, possibly introduced by a consideration of the picture on page 88. In what ways, if any, is it legitimate to use animals for sport?

c Discussion of cruelty. Why are people cruel to animals? Is this something that is inside every human being, or is it a defect in only a few? Is there any connection between cruelty to animals and callousness towards human beings? Why do the British give greater support to the RSPCA than to the NSPCC?

Some of these discussion points, of course pre-empt those given on page 96 of the pupil's book.

Using the story
The story has been presented with a large amount of explicit illustrative material to support the text, in order to make it as easy as possible for pupils to read it for themselves. Even slower readers should thus be able to gain a good grasp of both the framework and the detail of the story without too much help from the teacher. A straightforward use of the

story might, therefore, be:

1   Individual reading of the story.
2   Individual thought and possibly written answers (in rough) to the *Questions to think and talk about.*
3   Class discussion of these answers, followed by the *Discussion points.*

Alternatively, some of the work could be done in small groups:

1   Individual reading of the story.
2   Groups discuss the *Questions to think and talk about.*
3   Groups report back to the rest of the class. General discussion.
4   Groups discuss the *Discussion points.*
5   Reporting back and general class discussion.

In either case the work can be followed up by individual writing, based on the writing topics on page 96.

Approaches to criticism

Some teachers may wish to begin elementary critical work in the third year. Possible topics for discussion are suggested below. They are not presented in a form that can be given straight to the class. They are a series of guidelines, or suggestions about ways in which the story might be explored critically.

The Setting

The feelings we get about this part of Australia. How the author conveys this. How it affects the story as a whole.

Characters

Are the two pilots 'characters'? Are they distinguished from each other? To what extent are they defined as people? What insight do we get into the mind of the fighter pilot? What about the farmer? What is his character? Is he a character or a type?

Eagle(s)

What feelings does the writer give us about these birds at the beginning of the story? Do they change as it progresses? What picture do we get of the birds' appearance, size, movement, 'intelligence'? How is this achieved by the author?

Language and Imagery

The author's style is frequently poetic. He uses a lot of figurative language:

'. . . the earth below him and the creeks were brown and dry as a walnut . . .' Why is this so appropriate?

Find as many examples as you can of similar comparisons. Do any of these images recur? How successful are they?

Theme

Why did the author choose to write about this particular subject matter? What *is* the subject matter – killing birds, or the effect of war on men's minds? Is there a deliberate 'message'? If so, what?

Contents

FUTURE IMPERFECT

* Pupil's book page
** Teacher's book page

Analysis of activities

Discussion: 97   99   T41   T42   T43   T44
Writing: narrative   99   T42
        report   101
        in role   101   T42
        diary   T42
        exposition   111   T44
        dialogue   112   T45
        argument   112
        science fiction   T43
Comprehension: 101   111   T42
Appreciation: T45
Group work: T44
Research: 111   T42
Drama: T46

Illustration

Pupil's book page 97   discussion

The discussion of the two stills could progress towards a consideration of the ways in which our visions of the future do in fact reflect the way we see our own society; in particular our contemporary industry and architecture. Pupils might also like to think about what kind of story each of the stills illustrates.

The examination

Pupil's book pages 98–9   discussion

Discussion points
A *Examinations today*
1 Why do we have examinations?
2 How efficient are the exams at doing their job?
3 Can you think of better ways of doing the same thing?
B *Examinations in the future*
1 Do you think that in fifty years' time there will still be examinations as we know them now?
2 If not, why not?
3 If the examination system does change, in what ways do you think it *should* change?
C *Classifying people*
In this story the government obviously classifies the citizens of the country.
1 In what way do they want to classify all children?
2 Why do they do this?
3 Does our government classify people in any way?
4 If so, in what ways, and for what purposes does it do this?
5 Is it necessary to classify people?

To see the rabbit

Pupil's book pages **100–101**

writing; research; discussion

Writing

You are one of the people who went to see the rabbit. When you get home that day you write a diary in which you describe what happened and how you felt about it.

Research

Every year several species of life become extinct in Britain. Make a list of all the birds and animals you can find that have become extinct in Britain during the past fifty years.

Possible sources of information:

school library ⎫ *encyclopaedias and the section*
public library ⎬ *dealing with animals and birds*
school biology teachers ⎭

Discussion

Every year several species of life become extinct in Britain.

1 Does it matter?
2 If not, why not?
3 If it does, what should be done about it?

Ageless?

Pupil's book pages **102–3**

comprehension; writing; discussion

Comprehension

Questions A

1 At the beginning of the story, what are Lou and Em doing?
2 About whom are they talking?
3 How do they feel about him?
4 What is anti-gerasone?
5 Why do they want Gramps to stop taking anti-gerasone?
6 What does Gramps keep saying about giving it up?
7 In this story people are clearly very overcrowded and very heavily taxed. Why?
8 What does Emerald wish people would do?

Questions B
1 Why did Em's parents describe her marriage as being 'between May and December'?
2 What effect do you think it would have to dilute anti-gerasone?
3 What would Gramps do if he found Lou and Em 'tinkering with his anti-gerasone'?
4 Who do you think Verna and Melissa are?
5 Why are they unhappy?
6 For how long has Gramps been talking about 'leaving'?
7 When was anti-gerasone invented?
8 In what way does Lou sympathize with Gramps and his generation?

Questions C
1 In a few sentences describe the character of Gramps.
2 Explain briefly why Lou and Em want Gramps to die.
3 Explain the effects that the invention of anti-gerasone has had on society.
4 If you were a scientist and had just discovered the substance from which anti-gerasone was made, and realized the effects it could have, would you tell the world?

These three sets of questions are graded in ascending order of difficulty.

Writing
Write a conclusion for this story.

Discussion
Like many science-fiction stories, this one is based on an aspect of present day life. We live in what is sometimes described as an 'ageing society'. That is to say that the proportion of older people to younger is increasing.
1 Why is this?
2 What effects is it having on our lives?
3 What should we do in order to cope with it?
4 Is it necessarily a good thing to help people to live longer?

Life in the twenty-first century

Questions to think and talk about

1   In this society how do young people *learn*?
2   What do they learn?
3   Why are they not forced to go to school?
4   What is people's opinion of learning from books?
5   How does the old man 'prove' that school learning does not work?
6   How would you describe the two children in the shop and the way they behave towards their visitor?
7   What is the attitude of these people towards buying and selling?
8   What is their attitude towards private property?
9   How does the visitor react to all this?
10 What feature of this story strikes you as most

   a   strange
   b   realistic
   c   amusing

Group discussion

In this passage from *News from Nowhere*, William Morris is very critical of formal education.

1   Make a list of the reasons why he criticizes it.
2   How many of these points do you think are true?
3   Do you think that the kind of 'education' Morris describes would work?
4   What do you think would be an ideal education?

Writing about Utopia

A Utopia is an ideal world in which everything is perfect. People who have written about Utopias have usually done so to criticize bad features of the world they themselves live in.

A   *Morris' Utopia*
1   Make a list of the main features of Morris' Utopia mentioned in the passage.
2   List the features of his own world that you think he was criticizing.
3   Use these notes to write a short description of Morris' Utopia and the criticisms it contains.

B   *Your Utopia*
1   Make a list of the main features of our society that you dislike.
2   Make a list of the features of your Utopia that would replace these.
3   Write a description of your Utopia.

The pedestrian

Pupil's book pages 107–110

appreciation; writing; drama

Appreciation

The background
In this story the writer assumes that certain changes have taken place between the present day and the future date when the events he describes actually happen. Read the story through carefully and list the main changes that have taken place.

Character
For each of your answers in this section back up what you say by quoting from the story.

1 What impression do you get of Leonard Mead?
2 How does he 'fit in' to the society he lives in?
3 How does he behave when he is questioned?
4 Is he a brave man?
5 Why does he say at the end, 'That's my house'?

Future and present
Many science fiction stories have their starting point in the present: sometimes they are a criticism of the way things are now. The writer may take some aspect of present-day life and ask himself the question, 'If things go on like this, what will life be like in a hundred years' time?' Do you think that Ray Bradbury was criticizing life in his own time when he wrote this story? If so what aspects of it was he criticizing? Do you see any similar features in the world you live in?

Writing: dialogue

Much of this story is told in the form of a conversation between Leonard Mead and the police car. Write a story in which conversation plays a very important part. (You could even try writing a story which is told *only* through conversation.) Choose your own subject matter, or make up a story which includes one of the following pieces of dialogue:

A   'So you've come at last.'
    'What do you mean?'
    'We've been waiting for you.'
    'You mean you were expecting me?'
    'Of course.'

B   'There she goes again.'
    'Let's just watch her for a minute.'
    'It'll only be the same as before.'
    'Yes, I know.'
    'Then why don't we put an end to it?'

C   'Just calm down.'
     'But . . .'
     'If you could just calm down for a minute you'd be able to explain
     much better.'
     'That's all very well, but you don't understand.'
     'I'm trying to understand.'
     'No you're not. You're just sitting there laughing at me.'

Drama
The dialogue fragments in the writing exercise can be used as starting
points for improvized pair conversations. The following method works
well.

1   The pairs are given (on paper, or written up on the board) one
     dialogue.
2   They discuss who the two people might be; what they might be
     talking about.
3   They decide on the basic facts of their scene:
     who each is
     where the dialogue takes place
     when the dialogue takes place
     what it is about
     how it starts
4   They arrange any necessary furniture and then get into position to
     start.
5   All pairs begin to improvize at the same time. (To avoid awkward
     pauses.) They improvize the dialogue, preferably without having
     planned an ending. There is no need for them to use the exact words
     given – indeed it should be stressed that they should not attempt to,
     because otherwise they will keep stopping the flow of the scene to
     look at their pieces of paper, which is exactly what is *not* required.
6   Afterwards the class discusses the conversations that have been
     improvized. Some may wish to share theirs with the others, but there
     should be no pressure to do so.
The same method can then be used for further snippets of dialogue.

The knowledge explosion
Thinking and writing about the unit

Pupil's book pages **111–2**   organization

These pages can be used with the class as a whole, or as individual work,
for homework, etc.

Contents

BLUE HORIZONS

* Pupil's book page
** Teacher's book page

Analysis of activities

Discussion: 115   117   T51   T53   T55
Writing: language in use   115   126   127
　　　　　　 description   115   127   T54
　　　　　　 in character   115
　　　　　　 dialogue   T53
　　　　　　 newspaper/TV news report   T54
　　　　　　 letter   126   127
　　　　　　 opinion   128
Comprehension: 117   T52   T54
Word study: 128
Criticism: T52   T53   T54
Simulation: 124–127
Drama: T54
Group work: T55   T56
Research: 128

Illustrations

Pupil's book page **113**   discussion

This unit seeks to set a number of question marks against traditional and contemporary ideas about holidays – some serious, some light-hearted. The title page introduces the thematic material developed in the first two pages of text. It is increasingly taken for granted that the more visually interesting parts of the third world and the Mediterranean are fair game for the package tour operator. As Orwell argues forcefully, however, what may seem picturesque to the tourist is often the exhausting daily grind of poverty for the native inhabitant.

The material on this page is intended to show this visually. It doesn't matter that the particular 'holiday resort' depicted may be beyond the means of some people. It represents a genuine aspiration for many of us. If we accept the aspiration, even if we never achieve it, then the criticism implied by the contrast between the two photographs applies to us.

No discussion topics are presented in the pupil's book. Teachers are free to use the pictures as they wish. One possible approach is indicated below.

Questions to think and talk about

1 Would you like to have a holiday in the place shown in picture 1. Why?

2 Picture 2 was taken at much the same time as picture 1, and in the same country. How would you describe the way of life of these people?

3 If you had a holiday in Sicily, would it bother you to see scenes like that in picture 2?

4 Suppose you were one of the people in picture 2. What would you think and feel when you saw tourists in your country?

5 Do you think that the tourist industry brings any advantages to the inhabitants of places like Palermo?

Two views of Morocco

Comprehension

Questions A

1 Write three sentences of your own describing what Morocco is like according to the first piece of writing.
2 Write three sentences of your own describing what Morocco is like according to the second piece of writing.
3 Explain why the second writer thinks it is wrong for countries in Asia and Africa to be 'accepted as holiday resorts'.
4 Explain why the second writer thinks that people in hot countries are 'invisible'.

Questions B

1 Why does Orwell think that despite the poverty, countries in Asia and Africa are accepted as tourist resorts?
2 How does he contrast an Englishman's view of Morocco with the reality he sees himself?
3 He says that the land is cultivated with 'frightful labour'. Give one instance of this.
4 Describe in your own words the type of plough used, and explain why it is like this.
5 Describe in your own words the appearance of the old women carrying firewood.
6 What is the point of what Orwell says about donkeys?

Criticism

Compare the travel brochure with Orwell's writing, especially lines 7–10 and 19–27 of the Orwell piece. Both writers have the same subject matter and both have presumably visited the place they are writing about. Yet the way in which they write could hardly be more different.

1 What are the main differences between them?
2 *Why* are the two pieces so different?
3 Is one better than the other, or are they just different? If 'better', what do we mean by 'better'?

These exercises are presented in ascending order of difficulty. Questions A and B could be set as one exercise, or as one exercise (A) with supplementary questions (B) for those who finish more quickly. The exercise in criticism could be simply a written exercise, but is probably more useful as a class discussion, initially at least.

Rainbow

Pupil's book pages **116–7**   writing

Writing

As you read the story, try to get a clear picture of the characters of Ben, Sam and 'I'. Try to imagine what they would be like in other situations. Then write a brief conversation between the three of them in one of these situations:

Sightseeing while on holiday

At school when all three have got into trouble for some reason

Visiting Ben's rich uncle

Watching planes land at an airport

At the Motor Show

or choose a situation of your own.

Work and play

Pupil's book pages **118–9**   discussion; criticism

Questions to think and talk about

1   What opinion does the writer have about going to the seaside in summer?
2   What does he compare the holidaymakers with?
3   Who does he think is 'better off'?
4   Why?
5   Do you agree with him?

Comparisons

The poem contains a number of comparisons. For example it describes the swallow as 'a fish of the air'. The poet looks at the way the swallow moves through the air, in swift darts with rapid changes of direction. It reminds him of the movements of a fish in water, so he describes the swallow as 'a fish of the air'.

Find four other comparisons in the poem. Write them down. After each one explain what you think the poet had in mind when he wrote it.

The words *metaphor* and *simile* have deliberately been avoided here, although they can, of course, be introduced if it is thought appropriate. More important than the technical terms, however – especially at this early stage – is the ability to respond to images and to begin to talk about one's response.

Newsflash

Pupil's book page **119**   writing; drama

Writing
During the day more news comes in about these strange events. By evening it is possible to piece together what actually happened. Write the full story of what happened in the form of either a newspaper story, or a TV news report.

Role-play
Decide for yourself

a for what 'crime' these people have been arrested and
b what the French and German police are doing in Britain anyway.

Pair conversation 1
The French or German policeman reports to his boss about the arrests.

Pair conversation 2
The policeman interrogates one of the people he has arrested.

My happiest holiday

Pupil's book page **120**   comprehension; writing

Comprehension
Questions A
1 Why did David Garnett go to Russia?
2 Whom did he make friends with?
3 What did they teach him?
4 What did he like eating best?
5 Why did he think it was his best holiday?

Questions B
1 Was the area he visited fertile or not? How do you know?
2 What did the boys do about food at midday?
3 How did they show their generosity?
4 What was the main problem the people had to face?
5 What difficulties did David and his mother encounter on their journey to Tambov?

As before, the 'A' questions are easier than the 'B' set.

Writing
Write a description of a real or imaginary holiday that you feel was *your* 'happiest holiday'.

Indian country   Navajo children

Group discussion

This passage is best used after some introduction by the teacher. There are two reasons for this: the writing itself is not easy and some of the expressions might unintentionally cause confusion or offence in a multi-cultural classroom.

Both these pieces of writing are about Arizona, which is a popular tourist area of the south-western United States. It is the original home of the Hopi and Navajo Indians, and survivors of these two tribes still live in the area and form one of the 'tourist attractions'.

Like Orwell, Lawrence found the abuse of poor or 'primitive' societies as mere tourist attractions degrading. Hence his tone of scornful irony. The use of terms such as 'negress' and 'half-breed' was common at the time he was writing, but is not generally accepted today.

1   By the time Lawrence visited the area – in the 1920s – the Indian snake dance was already an attraction for tourists. How did Lawrence feel about
    a   the tourists in general
    b   the snake dance
    c   the attitude of Americans to this part of their country?

2   How would Lawrence have liked the Americans to treat the Indians and their parts of the country?

3   The poem was written some years after the description of the snake dance. In what ways have things changed, or have they stayed the same?

4   How do the Navajo children think about the tourists?

5   How does the poet feel about the incident?

The language of the poem

1   The poet takes care to describe the children's movements. Write down the words he uses to do this. Do they give you a clear picture of their actions?

2   Why does he say 'It's no joke'?

3   What does *reverently* mean? Why does he write that the children take the lollipops reverently?

4   What is a *totem*? So what does he mean by the phrase *sugar totem*?

5   What do you think he means by the last line?

6   What impact does the poem as a whole have on you?

Madeira Funchal

General

These four pages are written so that they can be used either by individuals or by small groups. If all the activities are used, the work on this section will occupy between five and eight 40-minute lessons.

Group work

There are general comments on small group activities in the *Introduction*. If this section is done in small groups, each of the writing exercises is preceded by a period of discussion and decision-making. This ends with the drafting of an agreed outline answer. The individual members of the group then use this as the basis of a piece of written work, incorporating their own views into their answer. In the case of the final activity *(Be a travel agent)*, the group begins as usual with discussion and planning. The different elements of the practical work can then be divided among members of the group. Work done can then be displayed on the wall or made into a folder that can be passed round to other groups.

Supplementary material

It is useful to get hold of a quantity of travel brochures for use when doing this section. At the end of winter and summer holiday seasons, travel agents are usually very happy to get rid of surplus brochures. These can be used for an introductory class discussion of the language and style of travel brochures. They can then be cut up for photographs when groups are working on *Be a travel agent*.

THE CHILDREN'S CRUSADE

Pupil's book pages 129–148

General

The Children's Crusade was first produced by the National Youth Theatre in 1973 and was the fruit of a collaboration between the actors, the director Ron Daniels, and the writer Paul Thompson. The music, some of which is printed at the end of these notes, was composed by Robert Campbell. The play was thus written specifically for young people and from its inception made specific provision for their creativity, especially through improvization. It is therefore very suitable for use with adolescents who have a little experience of, and interest in, improvized classroom drama. On the other hand, the themes it deals with: youthful idealism opposed to the betrayal and cynicism of an indifferent adult world, mean that even a classroom reading of the play will yield much that is valuable.

Structure of the unit

This unit consists of five major scenes from the play. After each scene there are brief suggestions about follow-up activities. These *are* brief for the good reason that the obvious thing to do with a play script is to act it, or at least read it aloud as dramatically as one can. Approaches to a class acting-out of the play are suggested below. The structure of the five scenes is as follows:

Scene 1
Characters: Pope Innocent III   6 Cardinals   Old Crusader
Setting: Two areas: **a** one larger one, possibly with different levels, for the Pope and Cardinals
   b a smaller separate one for the Old Crusader
Action: The dialogue between Pope and Cardinals expresses the attitude of the Church to the Crusades. The comments of the Old Crusader express the reality and cynicism of the 4th Crusade, from which he has just returned.
Style: Statuesque, formal, ritualistic.

Scene 2
Characters: Nicholas   Nicholas' father   Francis   Old Crusader
   Other parents, including a Mother
   Young people (developed through improvization):

Lesley	John	Colin	Patrick	Terry
Jane	Steve	Andrew	Trevor	Tony
Lindy	Michael	Jonathan	Robert	Paul
Debbie				

(These characters are worked out by the actors and they, and the relationships between them, remain constant through the play.)

Setting: A (central) area for Nicholas and Francis and the swearing-in ceremony. Other, smaller areas, for the short leave-taking scenes developed through improvization.

Action: Nicholas and Francis address the children and explain the Crusade. Children begin to come forward and take the vow of the Crusade. While this ceremony proceeds, we see individual scenes of parting and commitment. The scene ends with a song and a procession.

Style: Formal and ritualistic speech; then improvized; then formal movement.

Scene 3
Characters: Farmer   Klaus and David his sons   Simon
Setting: A general area representing one of the fields on the farm.
Action: A farmer is ploughing, using his sons as labour. One of the Crusaders, Simon, comes to beg for food. The younger son, David, is attracted to the idea of the Crusade. Seeing this, the farmer offers Simon far more food than he has asked for – *or* his son. Simon chooses David instead of the food.
Style: Naturalistic dialogue.

Scene 4
Characters: Nicholas   Francis

Other Crusaders developed through improvization:

Lindy	Trevor	Richard	Steve
Lesley	Peter	Ian	Patrick
Stephanie	Dennis	Andrew	
Caroline	John	Robert	
Bill	Paul	Pip	

Setting: A separate area for Nicholas. A number of small areas for short improvized scenes.
Action: The Crusaders arrive at the Alps. They are cold, tired, and hungry. It is night. Francis goes round trying to help and encourage them. Nicholas remains aloof and says that they must pray for help.
Style: At first formal movement (with song); then improvized; then naturalistic dialogue.

Scene 5
Characters: The Marquis of Montserrat   Francis   David   Nicholas
   Crusaders   Peasant Leader   Peasants
Setting: An open space.
Action: The Crusaders need food and shelter. Francis arranges that they will work on the estates of the Marquis of Montserrat. All seems to be

going well until some local peasants arrive. It becomes clear that the Marquis is using the children as cheap labour to avoid having to pay wages to the peasants. An angry argument ensues, but at last the peasants are forced to leave.

Style: Naturalistic dialogue interspersed with a section of stylized movement, and ending with a similar section.

Organizing work on the unit

As was suggested earlier, the natural thing to do with a play is to act it. The unit can, however, be used for play-*reading* – although inevitably some of the feeling of the scenes will be lost if this is done.

Reading the play

If it is decided to use the script for reading, then the suggestions after each scene will provide follow-up activities and encourage thought and speculation about the characters, relationships and subject matter of the scene.

Acting the play

The work can all be done by the class as a whole, or certain parts can be allocated to groups within the class. The extent to which this is practicable will depend on both the experience of the class and the space available. The scenes contain a variety of different dramatic styles and each demands a different kind of preparation:

FORMAL/RITUALIZED SPEECH

Here it is sufficient to organize an effective grouping of characters and then concentrate on *how* the speeches should be read.

STYLIZED MOVEMENT

This demands considerable practice. It is best to begin with a fairly naturalistic form of movement and then to work out ways to simplify the actions and fit them to a set pattern or rhythm. Given the space, this is something that a group of children can be left to work out on their own.

IMPROVIZED SCENES

These can be developed in small groups, even where space is limited. They are usually for twos, threes, or fours, and the sample dialogues in the script give the actors a clear idea of the kind of thing to aim for. The groups can discuss this and then try out a number of such scenes before choosing one to practise for inclusion in a class sequence of scenes. The ordering and positioning of these short dialogues can then be worked out in discussion with the class as a whole.

NATURALISTIC DIALOGUE

This presents more problems. It is probably best to go for the following form of rehearsed reading:

a the parts are cast

b the actors are given time to study their parts and think about how they will say them

c they can practise the scene without movement, to get a satisfactory interpretation

d they discuss how the scene should be mounted and work out a basic pattern of movements

e they then practise the scene with the movements that have been worked out.

This is not an ideal way of producing a scene in a play that is ultimately to be performed, but it is a useful way of focussing on this type of script and presenting it in the classroom.

The music

It is unlikely that most teachers will want to use the music in ordinary class work. The songs can be spoken, possibly chorally, certainly rhythmically. For those who would like to gain a clearer impression of what the final effect ought to be, however, Robert Campbell's music for the two songs is printed below:

The song of the confidence of youth

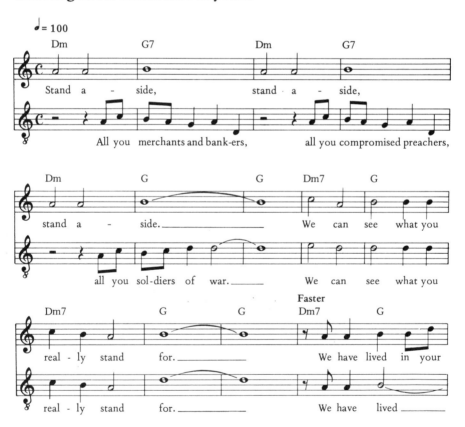

The song of overcoming difficulties

(to 2nd verse and then to 2nd CHORUS)

Slower

now we shall go hungry, But then a-gain that's just a no-ther fact.

food, go hungry, But then a-gain that's just a-no-ther fact.

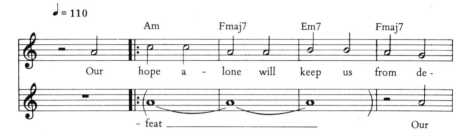

♩ = 110

Our hope a - lone will keep us from de -

- feat _____ Our

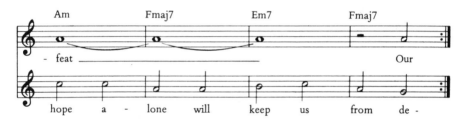

- feat _____ Our

hope a - lone will keep us from de -

Section B: Notes

Talking and writing
There are, inevitably, problems in presenting a section about talking and writing in purely written form. Ideally the class should hear the spoken material before seeing it on the page. It is very useful, therefore, to prepare tape recordings of spoken language to play to the class before embarking on this unit. If these are of a similar type to the material in the unit, so much the better:

a football commentary from the radio
a short piece of domestic conversation

In this unit the word 'sentence' is being used in two different ways. It is important that the distinction made in the text should be understood by the class.

A written sentence, which is defined in the traditional grammatical sense of a group of words making complete sense and containing a finite verb and, usually, a subject.

A spoken sentence, which corresponds to what is sometimes called an 'utterance'. This is a group of words that is complete and makes sense within the spoken context in which it occurs.

The actual terminology is less important than the realization by pupils that written and spoken language operate according to different rules. In the case of spoken language there is no need to discuss those rules, since in most cases children have been functioning very effectively in speech for years. Where problems occur is in the use of written language, the rules of which do sometimes have to be made explicit. A fruitful source of error lies in the confusion of spoken and written language: the child 'writes as he speaks', and what will work perfectly well in many speech contexts is not acceptable in writing and may even prove totally incomprehensible to the reader.

Moving from speech to writing
The previous unit focussed on the differences between spoken and written language and the fact that if these differences are not understood inefficient writing may result. This difference was explored partly through exercises involving the transformation of spoken sentences into complete written sentences. This unit looks at a more common way of turning speech into writing: making written reports on conversations. This is not intended as an introduction to reported speech in the traditional sense, but as one way into the writing of reports and summaries.

It would again be useful to introduce this unit with suitable recorded material. In this case suitable material would be:

a short conversation between two pupils

a general interest interview taken from a radio news magazine

These can be used as the basis for written reports. The class hear the tape two or three times and then write a short report on what they have heard. (The tape can possibly be replayed once more later so that they can check that they have not missed anything important.)

What you say and how you say it

We can define 'what you say and how you say it' in this way:

meaning
words and grammar
sounds

These three items are all affected by the context in which the speech takes place:

when and where
what is being talked about
anything else that is happening and affecting the speech
the relationship between speaker and audience
what the speaker is trying to achieve

For every situation defined in this way there are appropriate and inappropriate versions of 'what you say and how you say it'. What is appropriate obviously has to satisfy the requirements of suitable vocabulary and grammar. It has also to be in the right 'tone' for the situation. Here 'tone' is being used in two ways: literally as 'tone of voice', but also as attitude towards the audience defined in the choice of language and general approach to the subject matter. All this applies equally to written language, except that the element of sound is removed, to be replaced by the writing or printing system used.

This unit and the next are concerned with these ideas of suitability and tone. By the third year most pupils have already developed a fairly acute ear for tone – as anyone who does regular drama work with them will be able to vouch – but they often find it difficult to articulate what they perceive intuitively.

The unit could well be introduced by short taped extracts parallel to those at the beginning of the text. The questions that follow the two printed extracts can then be applied to the recordings instead.

Exercise 2 can be done as a spoken, rather than a written, exercise. The two news items can also be worked out through small group discussion rather than by individuals, and then performed to the rest of the class.

What you write and how you write it

The best simple examples of tone in written language tend to come from the mass media. The two newspaper examples, while dated, illustrate well the difference of approach between a mass circulation daily and the 'quality' end of the market. The exercises on these two pieces are intended to operate at two levels. The *Questions to think and talk about* work at the level of intuitive response to what is read. Exercises 1 and 2 set out to provide a more analytical approach. Exercise 1 should reveal that Extract B offers more facts per hundred words and uses shorter sentences. It also expresses a much stronger viewpoint. Exercise 2 should show that one of the ways in which B does this is by using simpler and stronger adjectives (rude, explosive, choking, bitter, as opposed to grim, deflationary, swingeing). Exercise 3 then gives pupils the chance to try out what they have perceived by imitating or parodying the style of the two papers.

Types of writing: narrative and descriptive
This unit continues the work of developing a critical vocabulary for use when considering one's own or other people's writing. Here the terms *narrative* and *descriptive* are used, while *argument* occurs on page 170. In between, different aspects of narrative and description are considered in more detail.

What kind of description?
This and the next unit explore the ways in which audience and subject matter affect the ways in which we write.

A is part of a poem by D. H. Lawrence.
B is taken from *Collins Guide to Bulbs*.
C is from *Dobie's Seed Catalogue*.

What kind of narrative?
The introductory material is all genuinely taken from school exercise books:
A: History
B: Science
C: Geography

Points of view
It is always a difficult matter to judge at what point the writing of arguments should be introduced. Usually the first two years are too early and it must be done by the end of the fourth year. (By argument is meant, of course, writing that involves the reasoned presentation of a case, not merely unsupported assertions.) The emphasis in this unit is on presenting the evidence to support one side of an argument: not on balance, or on dealing with possible objections to one's own line of thought.

In brief
Moving from speech into writing introduced the idea of writing a report on something one has heard or read. This is part of the preparatory work on summary writing, that has generally to be done in the fourth and fifth years. This unit introduces another related theme: abbreviation and note-taking. As far as possible the exercises are related to realistic situations.

The abbreviations

ITN	Independent Television News
BBC	British Broadcasting Corporation
AD	In the year of Our Lord (Latin: *Anno Domini*)
BC	Before Christ
TUC	Trades Union Congress
VC	Victoria Cross
i.e.	That is (Latin: *id est*)
etc.	And so on (Latin: *et cetera* – and the rest)
BA	Bachelor of Arts
USSR	Union of Soviet Socialist Republics

Exercise 2 provides a second chance to look at the different ways in which different school subjects and teachers require pupils to write. The use of abbreviations in different subjects can sometimes appear very idiosyncratic indeed.

The next two parts of the unit examine how book titles and newspaper headlines are also specialized types of abbreviation. Like letter abbreviations they depend on shared background knowledge, but in a different way. To use the abbreviation TUC effectively, the writer depends on his reader's knowing what the letters actually stand for – or at least what they mean. *The Last Days of Hitler* relies for its effectiveness as a title on the reader's knowing who Hitler was. *Vet Behind the Ears* not only requires the reader to know what a vet is, but also, to be fully effective, needs him to catch the play on words with the saying 'Wet behind the ears'. Newspaper headlines can operate in much the same way as the text on page 175 suggests.

Page 177 moves the topic more explicitly towards the making of notes. It takes the real-life line that notes are usually only meant to be understood by the writer. They can therefore be as cryptic as the writer likes, *provided he can understand them later when he needs to use them.*